Nomit AND Pickle
get active

C. E. Cameron

Clink Street

Published by Clink Street Publishing 2025

Copyright © 2025

First edition.

The author asserts the moral right under the Copyright, Designs and Patents Act 1988 to be identified as the author of this work.

All rights reserved. No part of this publication may be reproduced, stored in a retrieval system or transmitted, in any form or by any means without the prior consent of the author, nor be otherwise circulated in any form of binding or cover other than that with which it is published and without a similar condition being imposed on the subsequent purchaser.

ISBNs:
978-1-915785-65-7 - paperback
978-1-915785-66-4 - ebook

Dedicated to Lucy

Always in our thoughts

1975 - 2019

xx

Nomit and Pickle were on a mission to get active!

Nomit had said to Pickle that he wanted to try some fun sports and to get himself into shape.

Of course, Pickle wanted to be involved too.

So, Nomit booked a visit to a sports training camp with all the facilities. They were soon on the athletics field, trying out all the latest equipment and, of course, keen to look as professional as possible!

Pickle was desperate to show Nomit her excellent breaststroke. She was convinced it was her best stroke - bang on point, perfect execution, demonstrating textbook technique.

Nomit was doing his best to coach Pickle the correct frog leg kick, but with dismay could see that Pickle was unable to change from her own 'Pickle style' breaststroke.

Basically, one leg following the freestyle technique and the other leg vaguely mimicking the actual breaststroke kick!

Pickle then starts to swim faster than other swimmers in the swimming pool. These swimmers were professional with all the competitive gear, extremely serious and not taking much notice of Pickle.

This is until Pickle races ahead in her lane. Other athletes and spectators on the side started clapping and cheering for Pickle, even though those in the pool were just in training mode.

Nomit was looking super impressed! Although Pickle's swimming style was way off the correct stroke, she was in fact really fast and amazing everyone in the pool!

Nomit suggests moving to the cycling track.

They both try out their professional triathlon bikes. Nomit looks cool on his bike, however Pickle struggles to work out how to use the cleats on her pedals and shoes...

Pickle topples over!

Nomit rushes over to help Pickle - she is okay. Nomit is worried this is too challenging for Pickle... however, he has an idea!

Nomit suggests Pickle uses her old bike - the basket on the front, flag on the back, bell and 'go faster' stripes with bunting and more!

Even though all the little Pickle touches on her bike are not professional, she starts pedalling and she is fast!

Pickle is speeding around the track and leaving dust behind and in the faces of the professional cyclists... and Nomit too!

Pickle is delighted and her bike is screeching ahead around the track!

Time to try running!

Pickle of course does not have the preferred athletic style of running. Anything but! Pickle's style is outrageous! Pickle has flailing arms, all out of sync, head bobbing around, skipping, hopping and running all muddled together. However, it is fast, really fast!

Nomit cannot believe it - people around the track, spectators, other athletes, the bee, are all amazed and in shock. Nomit has an idea, he has spotted a flyer advertising the 'Bellaland Triathlon Relay Race', which is the next day.

"Let's enter, Pickle - we can win it!?"

"Why not," says Pickle, "I don't have the correct gear or proper equipment, but I don't mind!"

They enrol and get ready.

Time to train!

Nomit coaches Pickle...

It is the night before race day and Nomit and Pickle want to get their preparation just right.

Nomit and Pickle have a massage, eat their pasta and fruit and drink lots of smoothies and water, in their towelling robes.

Nomit is super competitive and continues to talk tactics. His flip chart has coaching tips and serious team talks.

For their race plan, Nomit has allocated Pickle the swimming and running legs of the race and Nomit has opted for the cycling section. They are both feeling very confident and focused.

However, Pickle does have a secret stash of mixed sweets, cakes and chocolates for herself, ready to munch on as a midnight feast – making sure the sweet box is hidden well away from Nomit's view!

Race day arrives!

Pickle starts really strongly.

Her stroke is chaotic, with lots of splash swamping the other swimmers. But it doesn't matter - she is so quick!

Pickle gets out of the pool first, ready to hand over the relay baton to Nomit.

Now it is Nomit's turn.

Nomit has a great lead, thanks to Pickle's start.
Nomit is looking strong, but then... disaster...
Nomit gets a puncture!

Nomit can't believe it - he has the bike upside down, all the equipment to fix the puncture, desperate to mend the bike as quickly as possible. However, haste is making Nomit make mistakes, oil everywhere and tools flying around.

Eventually Nomit fixes the bike with Pickle shouting and encouraging him on, alongside the other spectators.

Now it is time for Pickle to get ready and start running.

Now Pickle is on the track.

Pickle starts running. She holds the relay baton tightly with all her strength.

It looks like an impossible ask to get anywhere near the front.

The others are ahead in the distance and it is only a short run. Pickle just has to run as hard and as fast and as quickly as she can.

Pickle runs in her own 'crazy' style. It looks really messy and out of balance, but it doesn't matter – it is fast and she is gaining on them!

And then we see Pickle - a last, desperate dash for the line.

Pickle dips her head...

...and her pink bow claims Nomit and Pickle third place in the Triathlon relay!

On the podium!

Nomit and Pickle are podium winners!

Bronze medals!

They cannot believe it – lots of hugs, emotion and happy tears. Nomit is so proud of Pickle.

Pickle is so pleased to impress Nomit – she so wanted to help them win a medal, even if it was in her own, special style.

Nomit didn't mind how Pickle did it, he just wanted her to 'get involved and get active'.

Nomit & Pickle's – "Thought for the Day"

So, what had Nomit & Pickle learnt from their time getting active?

It's not just the winning,
it's the taking part
...in your own special way.

Nomit and Pickle now look forward to their next adventure...

www.ingramcontent.com/pod-product-compliance
Lightning Source LLC
LaVergne TN
LVHW070059080426
835508LV00028B/3456